ABERDEENSHIRE
LIBRARIES

WITHDRAWN
FROM LIBRARY

Scary Creatures
KILLER WHALES

Written by
John Malam

Created and designed
by David Salariya

BOOK ☐ HOUSE

Author:

John Malam studied ancient history and
archaeology at the University of Birmingham,
England, after which he worked as an archaeologist
at the Ironbridge Gorge Museum in Shropshire. He
is now an author specialising in information books
for children on a wide range of subjects. He lives in
Cheshire with his wife and their two young
children. Website: www.johnmalam.co.uk

Artists:

John Francis

Robert Morton

Mark Bergin

Carolyn Scrace

Richard Coombes

Series Creator:

David Salariya was born in Dundee,
Scotland. In 1989 he established The Salariya Book
Company. He has illustrated a wide range of books
and has created many new series for publishers in the
UK and overseas. He lives in Brighton with his wife,
illustrator Shirley Willis, and their son.

Editor: Stephen Haynes

Editorial Assistants:
Rob Walker, Tanya Kant

Picture Research:
Mark Bergin, Carolyn Franklin

Photo Credits:

t=top, b=bottom

Galina Barskaya/Fotolia: 27
Mark Bergin: 11, 18, 24
Cadmium: 12b
Lars Christensen/Fotolia: 13
Corel: 21
Nolie Gumapac/Fotolia: 25
Thomas Kitchin & Victoria Hurst/NHPA: 22
Xavier Marchant/Fotolia: 23
Mountain High Maps/© 1993 Digital
   Wisdom Inc.: 28–29
philippev/Fotolia: 26

Published in Great Britain in 2008 by
Book House, an imprint of
The Salariya Book Company Ltd
25 Marlborough Place, Brighton BN1 1UB

SALARIYA

A catalogue record for this book is available
from the British Library.

HB ISBN: 978-1-906370-14-5
PB ISBN: 978-1-906370-08-4

Printed in China

Visit our website at **www.book-house.co.uk**
for *free* electronic versions of:
You Wouldn't Want to be an Egyptian Mummy!
You Wouldn't Want to be a Roman Gladiator!
Avoid Joining Shackleton's Polar Expedition!
Avoid Sailing on a 19th-Century Whaling Ship!

Killer whale toying with a sea lion

Contents

Are killer whales fish?

Killer whales look like fish. Like fish, they live in the sea, have fins and flippers, and their bodies are **streamlined**. But killer whales are not fish! They are **mammals** – just like cats, rabbits and humans. Like all mammals, they are warm-blooded, breathe air with lungs, and give birth to live babies that drink milk from their mothers.

Whales, dolphins and porpoises belong to a group of sea mammals called **cetaceans** (from an ancient Greek word meaning 'sea monsters'). The killer whale is the largest of the dolphins.

X-Ray Vision

Hold the next page up to the light and see what's inside a killer whale.

See what's inside

Male killer whale
7 metres long

Hector's dolphin
1.5 metres long

Blue whale
30 metres long

Adult human
1.5–1.8
metres long

A killer whale attacks a sea lion, tossing it out of the water before catching it in its mouth.

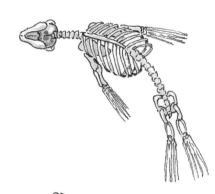

Sea-lion
skeleton

Did You Know?

The scientific name for the killer whale is *Orcinus orca*. People who don't like to call them 'killer whales' call them 'orcas' instead.

Skull

Killer-whale
skeleton

Spine or
backbone

Ribs

Flipper: note the 'finger bones' at the end of the flipper

What do killer whales eat?

Killer whales eat many animals, including other whales. They are the ocean's top **predator**. Adults eat about 250 kg of food every day – and not all of it comes from the sea. For example, they will snatch sea birds that settle on the water, and grab seals off beaches.

Did You Know?

Killer whales are known to eat land animals, such as moose (elk) and caribou (reindeer). The whales attack them as they swim across sea channels, moving from one feeding ground to another.

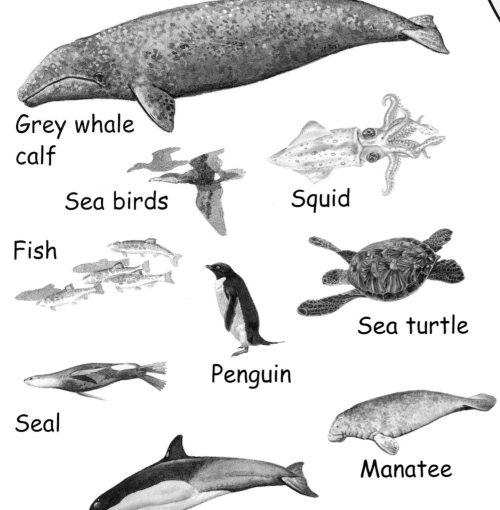

Grey whale calf

Sea birds

Squid

Fish

Penguin

Sea turtle

Seal

Manatee

Dolphin

Killer whales are not too fussy with their food. Their diet ranges from soft squid to tough turtles, small fish to giant whales. Scientists have either seen killer whales eating these animals, or found their remains inside the killer whales' stomachs. There's good news for humans – killer whales don't eat us!

How big is a killer whale?

Male killer whales are bigger than females. Adult males grow to about 7 metres long and weigh 5 tonnes, while females reach about 6 metres and 4 tonnes. Both males and females take around 10 years to grow into adults. Killer whales may be big, but many whales are bigger – the massive blue whale can be up to 30 metres long.

Killer-whale tooth

A killer whale's teeth are quite small. They are sharp and pointed, and curve backwards into its mouth. This is the best shape for holding on to and tearing at **prey**.

Did You Know?

An adult killer whale has between 40 and 56 teeth, each of which is about 7.5 cm long.

Flukes

Young whale (calf)

Adult female (cow)

Male killer whales are called **bulls**, females are **cows**, and young whales are **calves**.

Dorsal fin

Grey saddle-patch marking

Adult male (bull)

The saddle-patch marking behind the dorsal fin is different on every whale – just as all humans have different fingerprints.

Blow-hole

Eye

Eye patch

Pectoral fin or flipper

Males and females can easily be distinguished by the shape of their dorsal (back) fins. Male dorsals grow to 1.8 metres, and are upright. Female dorsals are smaller, at about 1.2 metres, and they usually curve backwards.

Female

Male

How fast is a killer whale?

Killer whales are the fastest members of the whale family, with a top speed of about 50 kph (their 'cruising speed' is about 10 kph). Their bodies are streamlined, like torpedoes. A smooth shape helps them move more easily through the water.

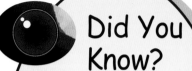

Did You Know?

Killer whales are not the fastest animals in the sea – that record belongs to the sailfish, which swims in bursts of up to 110 kph. Human swimmers can only manage a top speed of about 8 kph.

A killer whale swims by moving its powerful tail up and down through the water. The harder it 'beats' its tail, the faster it swims. It changes direction by moving its pectoral fins.

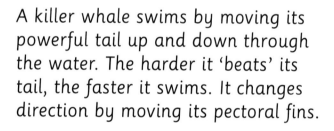

Pectoral fins

Lobtailing (above) is when a killer whale lifts its tail clear of the water, then slaps it down to make a loud splash. It does this when hunting, forcing fish to swim towards others in its group.

Sometimes killer whales lie on their sides and splash the water surface with their pectoral fins. This is called **flippering**. Perhaps they do this to send signals to other killer whales.

Killer whales are sociable animals. Sometimes they leap out of the water, in a display to others in their **pod** (family group). This is called **breaching**.

How long can a killer whale hold its breath?

Killer whales are air-breathing animals and come to the surface to fill their lungs. A killer whale breathes through a blow-hole on the top of its head. When it dives, it closes its blow-hole and holds its breath. Adults usually stay underwater for 5 to 10 minutes. But on deep dives, down to 30 metres, they can hold their breath for as long as 15 minutes.

A killer whale breathes out stale air through its blow-hole, making a **spout** of water droplets. Then it breathes in to refill its lungs with air.

Their lungs now filled with air, a pair of killer whales prepare to dive below the surface, where they will carry on foraging for food. The male has the tall, upright dorsal fin; the female has the shorter, curved fin.

Did You Know?

Baby killer whales are born underwater. The first thing they do is to swim to the surface to fill their lungs with air. As they swim up, they keep their blow-holes tightly closed.

Killer whales have black backs and white bellies. These are camouflage colours that help to break up the whale's outline, making it harder for prey animals to spot the whale as it moves towards them.

How do killer whales hunt?

Killer whales hunt in family groups or pods. They are known as the 'wolves of the sea', because wolves also hunt in packs. To find prey, the whales make clicking sounds, then listen for echoes as the clicks bounce off fish, seals and other animals. They can tell from the echoes what kind of prey it is. When the whales have located prey, they swim around it, herding it into a small circle. This makes it easier to attack.

Did You Know?

In the Antarctic, pods of killer whales knock sleeping seals and penguins off ice sheets, then catch them as they fall into the sea.

Finding prey by sound is called **echolocation**. It means that killer whales don't need to see their prey. This is useful at night and in deep or murky water.

Outgoing clicks

Incoming echoes

Shoal of fish

Killer whales on the hunt

Killer-whale skin is smooth and rubbery. It is coated in oil, which helps it slide quickly through the water. Unlike land mammals, whales do not have hair or fur. Instead, just under the skin is a thick layer of fat known as **blubber**. The blubber layer helps to keep heat in, even in freezing polar waters.

The pointed teeth of a killer whale can easily puncture the skin of a seal. Because the teeth point backwards, the seal finds it hard to free itself from the whale's grip. The killer whale might 'play' with the seal, using its mighty tail like a bat to knock its lifeless body high into the air. When playtime ends, the whale eats the seal.

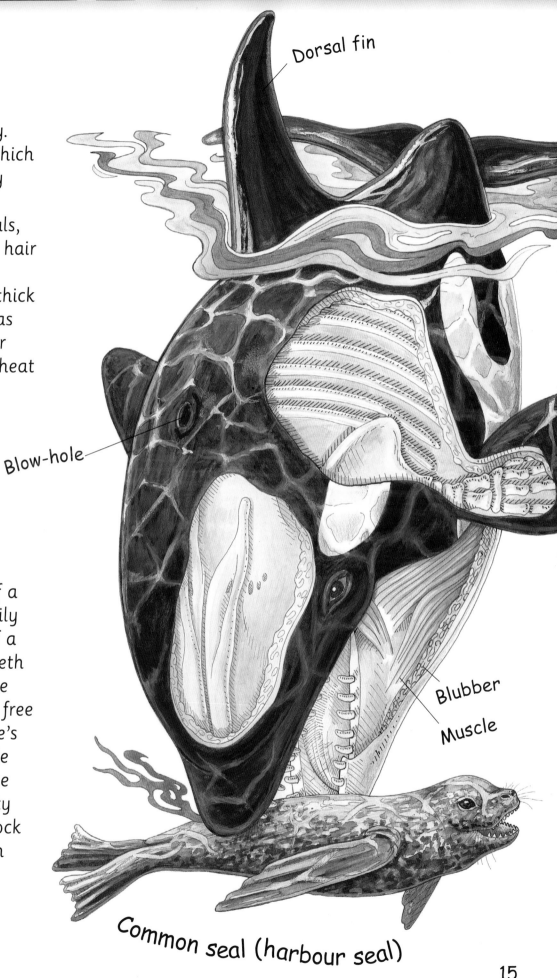

Dorsal fin

Blow-hole

Blubber

Muscle

Common seal (harbour seal)

How long does a killer whale live?

A baby killer whale is inside its mother's body for about 15 months before it is born. If it survives its first few months, it may have a long life ahead of it. Females often live for 80 to 90 years, but males are lucky if they reach 50.

When a calf is born, it comes out tail-first. It can weigh up to 200 kg and measure about 2.5 metres long. Within seconds, its mother guides it to the surface with her flippers and it takes its first breath of air. After half an hour, the baby can swim unaided.

Killer-whale calf

The mother feeds her calf with milk, which she squirts into its mouth. The calf stays close to its mother, always swimming close by her side. When it is about two years old, it starts to move away and hunt for solid food with the rest of the pod.

Did You Know?

Killer whales kept in zoos and water parks do not live as long as whales in the wild. Even calves born in **captivity** have shorter lifespans than their wild relatives.

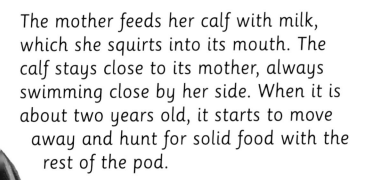
Female killer whale

Who lives in a killer-whale family?

Killer whales live their whole lives in a family group or pod. It's made up of mothers and their calves. As mothers give birth to new calves, these become half-brothers and half-sisters to the older calves. The fathers come from a different pod altogether, where they live with their mothers.

X-Ray Vision

Hold the next page up to the light and see what's under the water.

See what's inside

Spy-hopping

Orca pod

A pod has 10 to 20 whales in it, headed by a senior female.

Killer whales can 'stand' on their tails, poking their heads above the surface of the water. It's called **spy-hopping**, and they do this when they want to have a good look around.

Several generations of a killer-whale family live together – children, parents, grandparents and even great-grandparents.

Who studies killer whales?

The best place to study killer whales is in the wild, where they can be seen behaving naturally. Scientists spend years studying individuals and pods, watching them from boats, swimming alongside them, and following their travels with the help of space satellites. They also listen to and record their clicks and calls. All this is important work, helping us to learn about the lives of these wonderful whales.

Scientists can keep track of a killer whale by fitting it with a radio tag. Satellites can then plot its location.

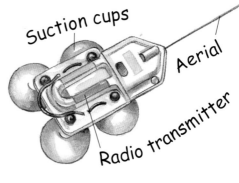

Suction cups

Aerial

Radio transmitter

Individual killer whales can be recognised by their dorsal fins. They are all slightly different shapes, and may have nicks along their edges.

What is whale-watching?

When tourists travel out to sea to look at whales, they are whale-watching. They use all kinds of boats, from small rubber inflatables that carry just four or five people, to large boats that take hundreds of people. Sometimes the whales are nowhere to be seen – but tourists who do see killer whales in the wild always say how exciting it is to watch them. If the whales spy-hop around the boats, they are people-watching!

Killer whales seem to enjoy being close to humans. They put on displays of breaching, lobtailing, flippering, spy-hopping and spouting.

Tongue

A killer whale's tongue is short and strong with a movable tip. It pushes food towards the whale's throat.

Are killer whales in danger?

Killer whales have never been hunted in large numbers by whalers, and there could be as many as 100,000 of them in the sea. But they are at risk from pollution, and they sometimes get trapped in fishing nets. In some places fishermen have used guns and explosives to wipe out entire pods, blaming them for eating too much fish.

Killer whales have been kept in captivity since the 1960s. Nearly all of them have been taken from the wild; very few have ever been born in zoos or water parks. A killer whale taken from the sea loses contact with its pod, which is bad for both the whale and its family group.

Look at the dorsal fin on this killer whale. Can you see how it's bent over? It should be upright. When a dorsal fin collapses like this, it shows the killer whale is stressed and unhappy. A killer whale taken from the sea will only live for about five years in captivity.

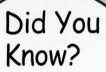

Did You Know?

Keiko was a killer whale caught near Iceland in 1979. He was put on show in Iceland, Canada and Mexico. In 1993 he starred in the film *Free Willy*. In 2002 he was released into the sea, but he no longer knew how to survive in the wild, and died the following year.

What do you think?

About 150 killer whales have been taken out of the wild, then kept in tanks or pools and made to perform tricks for audiences. Do you think it is right to do this?

How does pollution harm killer whales?

A killer whale's worst enemy is man. This is not because killer whales are hunted or captured, but because their natural **habitat** is being poisoned by toxic chemicals (toxins). Some toxins are deliberately dumped at sea, but others get there by accident. Although seawater dilutes the toxins and spreads them far and wide, they still find their way into the bodies of killer whales. Today, killer whales are the world's most contaminated whales.

Oil spilt accidentally from ships can be just as dangerous to sea creatures as poisons that are dumped on purpose. Other toxins may be washed into the sea from streams and rivers.

Once the toxins are in the sea, there is no way to take them out. They enter the food chain and eventually end up inside killer whales.

Did You Know?

Killer-whale mothers with toxins in their bodies can pass the poisons to their young. While the babies are inside their mothers, toxins pass into them through the bloodstream. After they are born, toxins are passed to the young through their mothers' milk. This makes them more vulnerable to disease.

How does a food chain work?

Animals eat plants or other animals, then they themselves get eaten by something else; this is a food chain. At the bottom of the chain is plankton – a mass of tiny plants and animals that drift in the sea. Plankton absorbs the toxins that are in the water. Then the plankton is eaten by shrimp-like creatures called krill, and the toxins pass into their bodies. When krill are eaten by squids, seals, penguins and other animals, the toxins are passed on. At the top of the food chain are killer whales. Toxins enter their bodies when they eat squids, seals and penguins.

Why are toxins dumped at sea?

Toxins are often dumped at sea because this is cheaper than disposing of them safely on land. Some people think that poisoning the sea does not matter because humans do not live there. Others think you don't need to worry about things you can't see. But the sea and its creatures are part of our own food chain as well.

Cetaceans around the world

Whales, dolphins and porpoises are found in all the world's oceans and seas. Some are long-distance travellers, but others spend their whole lives in one part of the world.

North America

Atlantic Ocean

Pacific Ocean

South America

Humpback whale
Found: Most oceans
Length: 13 metres
Weight: 30 tonnes

Minke whale
Found: Most oceans
Length: 8 metres
Weight: 12 tonnes

Sperm whale
Found: Most oceans
Length: 18 metres
Weight: 50 tonnes

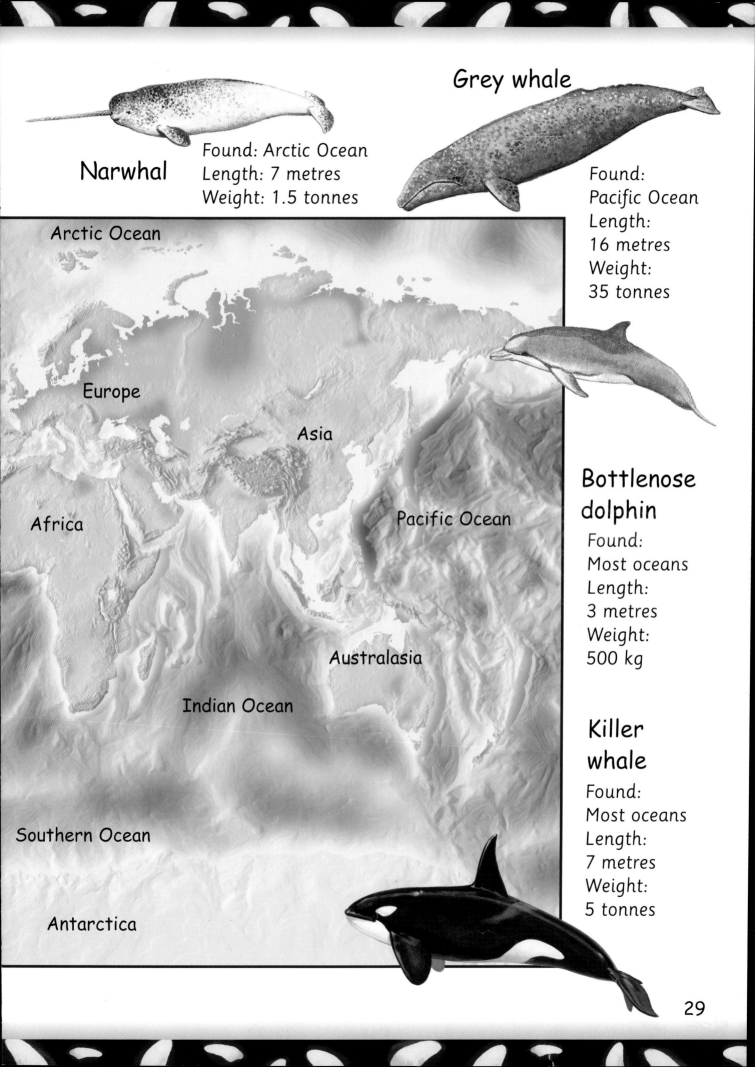

Narwhal

Found: Arctic Ocean
Length: 7 metres
Weight: 1.5 tonnes

Grey whale

Found:
Pacific Ocean
Length:
16 metres
Weight:
35 tonnes

Arctic Ocean

Europe

Asia

Africa

Pacific Ocean

Australasia

Indian Ocean

Southern Ocean

Antarctica

Bottlenose dolphin

Found:
Most oceans
Length:
3 metres
Weight:
500 kg

Killer whale

Found:
Most oceans
Length:
7 metres
Weight:
5 tonnes

Killer-whale facts

Most scientists believe that there is only one species of killer whale, but there are different groups. American and Canadian scientists found three different groups in the Pacific Ocean.

'Resident' killer whales live near the coast and feed mainly on fish.

'Transient' killer whales travel about more and feed mainly on marine mammals such as seals. Sometimes they will refuse to eat fish, even when there is nothing else to eat.

'Offshore' killer whales live far from land. They eat fish as resident whales do, but they travel in larger pods.

Killer whales were given their name long ago by whale hunters who saw them feeding on the bodies of dead whales. They called them 'whale killers', but over time the name has been switched round to become 'killer whales'.

When a killer whale closes its mouth, its top and bottom teeth lock together. This helps the whale to grip large prey and tear it into smaller pieces for easier swallowing.

In the early 1970s the United States Navy trained killer whales to dive to the seabed to recover lost objects such as torpedoes. They went as deep as 260 metres.

Each pod of killer whales has its own 'language' of clicks. This helps the whales to keep in touch with their pod, and not wander off to another group.

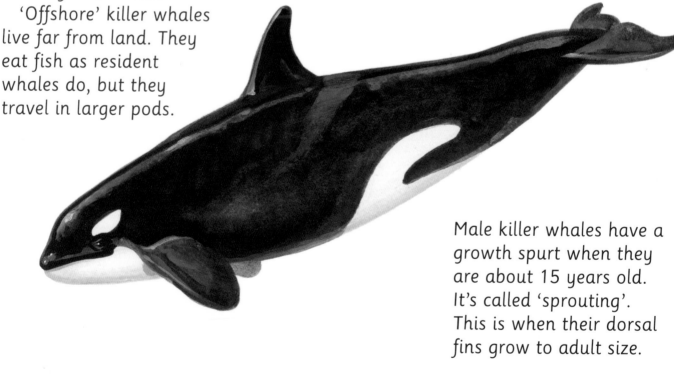

Male killer whales have a growth spurt when they are about 15 years old. It's called 'sprouting'. This is when their dorsal fins grow to adult size.

Glossary

beach rubbing Rubbing the body against pebbles in shallow water.

blow-hole The nostril or breathing hole on the top of a whale's head.

blubber The thick layer of fat just under a whale's skin.

breaching Leaping out of the water, then landing with a splash.

bull An adult male killer whale.

calf A young whale.

captivity The state of living in a human-made environment, such as a zoo.

cetaceans The group of animals to which whales, dolphins and porpoises belong. The word means 'sea monsters'.

cow An adult female killer whale.

dorsal fin The fin on the back of a whale or fish.

echolocation Making sounds and listening to the returning echoes. Whales and bats use this to find food and to navigate.

flippering Slapping a flipper onto the surface of the water.

flukes The two fins of a whale's tail.

habitat The natural environment in which a plant or animal lives.

lobtailing Slapping the tail onto the surface of the water.

mammal An animal that breathes air with lungs, is warm-blooded, gives birth to live young and feeds them on mother's milk.

pectoral fins Front fins or flippers.

pod A family of whales that live together.

predator Any animal that hunts other living creatures for food.

prey Any animal that is hunted by other animals for food.

saddle patch A light-coloured patch behind the dorsal fin of a killer whale.

spout A misty spray of stale air blown out through the blow-hole.

spy-hopping Lifting the head out of the water to have a look around.

streamlined Having a smooth shape that can move through air or water easily.

31

Index